Original title:
Beneath the Melon Sky

Copyright © 2025 Creative Arts Management OÜ
All rights reserved.

Author: Atticus Thornton
ISBN HARDBACK: 978-1-80586-445-5
ISBN PAPERBACK: 978-1-80586-917-7

Enigmas of the Cotton Candy Sky

A pink fluff whispers in the air,
Traces of laughter everywhere.
Clouds like sugar, oh so bright,
They giggle softly, day to night.

The sun's a giant jellybean,
It bounces high, it's quite the scene!
As twilight tickles the horizon low,
Candy rainbows start to glow.

Veils of Twilight's Glow

The moon wears shades, it's quite the sight,
It dances swiftly, just for flight.
Stars join in with twinkling grins,
Like fireflies sporting party spins.

A cat on a roof plays a sweet tune,
Beneath the antics of a playful moon.
Laughter bounces in the cool breeze,
As shadows skip among the trees.

The Sweetened Symphony of Dusk

Balloons drift up from every park,
Musical chairs with a playful spark.
The crickets croon a merry song,
While fireflies flicker, dancing along.

Cakes float by on marshmallow winds,
The world is silly, where joy begins.
Chasing shadows, we twirl about,
In a vibrant mix of giggles and shout.

A Dreamer's Canvas under the Stars

A brush of dreams paints the night,
Whimsical creatures take to flight.
With a sprinkle of mischief in the air,
Laughter bubbles, whimsical and rare.

Puddles reflect a chuckle in time,
As giggles linger, pure and sublime.
We dance with wishes, swirling around,
In a world where giggles abound.

Whispers of the Twilight Orchard

Apples giggle as they sway,
Laughter ripples through the day.
Cherries chase the bumblebee,
And dance around the old oak tree.

Squirrels play tag on branches high,
While sunbeams flirt and pass by.
The breeze tells secrets to the leaves,
In this orchard, joy never leaves.

Shadows Cast by Summer's Embrace

Lemons tell jokes in the sun,
While watermelons have their fun.
Peaches roll and laugh out loud,
They're the silliest in the crowd.

Cucumbers wearing shades of green,
Are the cool kids, if you know what I mean.
Tomatoes giggle, red as can be,
Their humor ripe, oh so fruity!

Beneath the Citrus Veil

Oranges joke with zesty glee,
While limes are sour as can be.
Grapefruits wear hats made of rind,
In this realm, laughter's well-defined.

Pineapples gossip, spiky and bright,
Under the stars that twinkle at night.
Their tales of summer's wild spree,
Are shared with glee, joyfully free.

Melodies of a Dusk Horizon

As twilight hums a funny tune,
Ripe berries dance beneath the moon.
Kiwis croon in delightful cheer,
Their fruity songs, we all hold dear.

Strawberries strut in stylish hats,
While blueberries leap like acrobats.
Each sunset brings a playful jest,
In this patch, we laugh the best.

The Colors of a Dreaming Heart

In a land where the rabbits wear bowties,
And the clouds are made of marshmallow pies,
Dancing sunflowers clap their green hands,
While jellybeans rain on the bright strands.

A fish in a suit plays the saxophone,
As butterflies play chess on a purple throne,
Laughter bubbles like soda, so sweet,
In this whimsical world where daydreams meet.

The cows strut around with sunglasses on,
And the grass sings a tune at the break of dawn,
The squirrels juggle acorns with ease,
While ladybugs play cards under the trees.

Giraffes wear hats at a fancy event,
While popcorn flocks line up for a tent,
With smiles on their faces, as bright as can be,
In a color-filled world that's silly and free.

Floating on a Breeze of Warmth

A kite in the sky yells, 'Catch me if you can!',
While ants in bowler hats organize a clan,
Rubber ducks float in a stream of giggles,
Their laughter ripples, as the sunshine wiggles.

Happiness drizzles like syrup on toast,
While the winds tell tales of what matters most,
A cloud shaped like a cat yawns wide and bright,
Inviting us all for a soft, fluffy flight.

Ice cream cones climb trees with such flair,
While woeful old socks dance without a care,
The breezes play tag, as we chase them around,
In a world where all joys silently abound.

With each gust that tickles our cheeks with delight,
A dragonfly whispers secrets in flight,
We twirl through the day on a sea of warm air,
In a merry parade of laughter to share.

Twilight Tales of Celestial Journeys

The stars come out wearing glittery shoes,
While the moon smiles down, sharing silly news,
Comets race past, tripping on their tails,
As planets play tag with whimsical trails.

A hedgehog astronaut floats in a dream,
Sipping stardust from a candy cane stream,
Celestial critters sing songs of delight,
Under a quilt of soft twinkling light.

Meteor showers spill popcorn so sweet,
While aliens tap dance with three tiny feet,
Galaxies tumble in funny old spins,
As laughter erupts where the stardust begins.

The sun winks cheekily at the deep blue night,
As fireflies twinkle, taking center stage light,
Each story they share brings a chuckle or cheer,
In twilight's embrace, we find joy far and near.

Echoes from the Orchard's Heart

In an orchard full of cheer,
Apples giggle, quite near.
Pears doing the twist and shout,
While the cherries dance about.

Lemonade laughs by the tree,
Squirrels sip happily.
Turnips try to join in line,
But they tumble, oh so fine!

Peaches prance in bright sun rays,
Claiming they're the best at plays.
With a wink and cheeky grin,
They rove free – let the games begin!

The wind joins in this delight,
Causing branches to take flight.
Beneath the rustling leaves' glee,
Life is a dance, wild and free!

Twilight's Sweet Confection

The sky swirls like a candy treat,
While fireflies wiggle, oh so sweet.
Cotton candy clouds up high,
Swaying gently, float on by.

A giggling breeze tickles my nose,
Dancing petals in a row.
The daisies chuckle with delight,
As stars peek out, blinking bright.

Frogs croak their tunes, quite loud,
While crickets chirp, proud in the crowd.
The moon, a marshmallow so round,
Sends giggles fluttering all around.

In this twilight, laughter spins,
Sweets abound where joy begins.
A magical feast without a fuss,
As the sky twinkles just for us!

Beneath the Harvest Moon

Under the glow of a big bright orb,
Pumpkins laugh – how absurd!
Corn does the cha-cha on its stalk,
While ghosts sneak in for a walk.

Apple pies float by in a race,
Cinnamon rolls joining the chase.
With giggles of wheat in the hay,
Harvesting smiles in funky play.

The moon pulls pranks on the shy stars,
Making them twinkle like candy bars.
A scarecrow strikes a funny pose,
While falling leaves burlesque in rows.

With laughter mingling in the air,
Nature's jokes fly everywhere.
This harvest night—what a spree,
Life is a comedy, wild and free!

Serenity in the Swaying Branches

The branches sway in merry tunes,
Tickling leaves like playful tycoons.
A gentle breeze sings sweetly soft,
As birds join in with a chirpy loft.

Banana peels roll in the grass,
Apples snicker as they pass.
Oranges juggle in the air,
Laughing as they land with flair.

Even the sun, in its golden hue,
Winks at clouds, enjoying the view.
In this orchard of giggles and glee,
Nature's joy is wild and free!

As night wraps the world in a glow,
Stars laugh at the daytime show.
Serenity flows in light-hearted prance,
Inviting all to join the dance!

Splendor in the Haze of Evening

The sun dips low, a golden tease,
As shadows stretch like silly cheese.
A raccoon twirls in twilight's gleam,
Wearing a hat—a fashion dream!

Crickets chirp a funny tune,
They think they'll dance beneath the moon.
A firefly, with flair so bright,
Flashes like a beacon, what a sight!

The breeze whispers secrets to the trees,
Calling out to buzzing bees.
A squirrel performs acrobatic tricks,
Happily munching on nutty snacks.

All laugh and play in evening's glow,
As the world turns soft and slow.
In this odd, whimsical parade,
Laughter echoes, fears do fade.

Secrets Lurking in Sunset's Embrace

The sky is painted orange and pink,
A raccoon winks, what do you think?
A cat in sunglasses struts with pride,
As laughter swells, no room to hide.

A turtle takes its time to race,
Wondering if it's a flying saucer's place.
A rumor spreads among the weeds,
That ants are planning hilarious deeds.

The clouds float by like fluffy sheep,
Whispering giggles as the sunset creeps.
A toad croaks jokes near the pond,
With punchlines that tease and respond.

So secrets linger in hues divine,
While the day begins to recline.
With chuckles echoing through the air,
Every creature joins the evening fair.

The Auras of Enchanted Evenings

Evenings swirl in magic light,
With giggling squirrels taking flight.
A dancing shadow starts to prance,
Forgetting it's a nighttime dance!

Stars appear, a flashy crowd,
While owls hoot their sonnets loud.
A dragonfly spins tales to share,
Of silly things from everywhere.

A breeze, mischievous as can be,
Steals hats from folks who watch the spree.
The moon rolls by like a lazy ball,
In this enchanted evening hall.

So savor the laughter on the air,
In this magic, joy's everywhere.
With every wink of nighttime's eye,
Fun and folly soar and fly.

Celestial Reveries in Soft Hues

Midnight snacks with stars so bright,
A comical show, a cosmic delight.
A comet sneezes, leaving trails,
While friendly meteors tell tall tales.

The moon's a jester, spinning round,
With laughter echoing off the ground.
A spaceship lands with a clumsy thud,
As aliens giggle at the muddy flood.

Soft hues whisper secrets sweet,
Of floating dreams and dancing feet.
A bear in pajamas sips hot tea,
Sharing jokes with his grassy spree.

As night unfolds with warmth and cheer,
Laughter's melody fills the sphere.
In celestial realms, joy does bloom,
And silliness brightens every room.

A Wonderland of Warm Embraces

In a land where giggles bloom,
Each flower's a balloon in full zoom.
The trees tell jokes in rustling whispers,
While squirrels dance with acorn flippers.

Chubby clouds drift with candy canes,
As rabbits skateboard down the lanes.
Tickled by wind, they leap and bound,
In this silly space, joy is found.

A river flows with bubble gum,
While frogs croon songs, all off-beat and dumb.
The sun sports shades and a goofy grin,
While friends gather 'round, ready to spin.

So come, take a stroll through this land,
Where every mishap is perfectly planned.
Giggles and chuckles fill the air,
In a wonderland where we shed our care.

Glimmers of Stardust on Velvet Wings

Butterflies wear polka-dotted hats,
And dance with giggling acrobatic cats.
While fireflies play tag 'round the moon,
Their twinkling light makes silly tunes.

Stars play hopscotch in velvety skies,
With each jump, they let out funny sighs.
Planets roll dice, each pick a name,
And comets race, all in the game.

The evening breeze has a playful chat,
With whispers of laughter, his favorite hat.
As the night unfolds, dreams take flight,
Wrapped in sparkles beneath soft starlight.

In this topsy-turvy universe wide,
Galaxies swirl on a cosmic slide.
With stardust laughter floating around,
We celebrate joy that knows no bound.

The Enchantment of Astral Gardens

In gardens where the odd things grow,
Marshmallow bushes put on a show.
Lollipop flowers twist and twirl,
And giddy gnomes begin to swirl.

Bubbles float by with laughter inside,
While unicorns hop on a wobbly ride.
Each petal quivers with stories to tell,
Of mischievous sprites ringing a bell.

A rainbow twirls, bursting with cheer,
Sprinkling giggles as it draws near.
With snickering sprites, they play chess,
Crafting plans that lead to pure mess.

So wander through this whimsical plot,
Where happiness grows in every spot.
With each step taken in this odd land,
You'll find joy that's simply unplanned.

Where the Horizon Sings

On the edge where colors blend,
A panorama where laughter bends.
The sun throws jokes to the dancing trees,
While the breeze tells tales with giggling ease.

Clouds come by on a silly ride,
Wearing shades while the mountains slide.
As seagulls squeal in high-pitched tunes,
The waves clap hands under cartoon moons.

In this realm, where horizons play,
A ticklish tick-tock makes time sway.
The stars wink down with giddy surprise,
Mixed with smiles from the wide open skies.

So take a leap in this jolly place,
Where the horizon wears a silly face.
With every note that the landscape brings,
You'll find the joy in all it sings.

The Palette of a Sugar-Coated Dawn

In a world where candy clouds play,
A minty breeze lifts spirits high.
Jellybean trees in bright array,
Squirrels dance as lollipops fly.

Banana peels cover the ground,
With giggles echoing through the air.
Every step makes laughter abound,
As toasted marshmallows faintly glare.

Cotton candy fills up the streams,
As sugar sprinkles fall like rain.
Chasing dreams wrapped in whipped creams,
Silly hats bobble, causing pain.

Fairy floss floats, a billowy sight,
With chocolate rivers flowing wide.
This morning's silliness feels so right,
As all our joys take a wild ride.

Under the Warmth of Golden Spheres

With laughter bursting all around,
The sun wears smiles, shiny and bright.
Frogs in bow ties make a sound,
As they leap under the light.

Giggling flowers sway and twirl,
Puppies waddle in their sweet, soft coats.
Curly fries dance, oh what a whirl,
As ketchup squirts from playful boats.

Sprinklers sing a splashy tune,
While dancing ants parade in lines.
Chasing light from the sun at noon,
Each step triggered by silly signs.

Giggles ring through every ray,
A joyful pop on this fine day.
Silly moments weave along the way,
As sunshine smiles in a quirky ballet.

The Celestial Carousel of Colors

Round and round the stars unfold,
Giggling planets spin with glee.
A carousel of colors bold,
As silly comets zoom carefree.

Riding rockets, whooshing fast,
Moon pies flip with a silly sound.
A snack parade that'll surely last,
With fizzy drinks that swirl around.

Galaxies wink like playful cats,
Twinkling with mischief in their stride.
Meteors wearing silly hats,
Creating chuckles far and wide.

This cosmic show of hues and flair,
Brings laughter to our starlit dance.
Through colorful realms, we declare,
Life's a joke, so let's take a chance!

Sipping the Sweetness of Dusk

As the sun dips low, we pour,
Lemonade rivers fill our cups.
Giggles linger, oh what a score,
With cookie crumbs and silly pups.

The sky's painted with sugary dreams,
Candy bats fly on a fluffy breeze.
Marshmallow clouds play in moonbeams,
Leaving giggles hung like sweet teas.

Chasing fireflies, we blur the line,
Between what's real and just a jest.
Sipping sweetness feels divine,
In this twilight, we're all a fest!

As stars bloom in the dusky hue,
Laughter wraps around our delight.
This sugary sip, a sparkly view,
Turns evening's peace into pure light.

Shadows Dance in Pomegranate Light

In the twinkling glow of night,
The shadows jump, what a sight!
They twirl and spin with silly glee,
Chasing fireflies, wild and free.

A squirrel joins, a dance so bold,
In paws, acorn treasures to hold.
They giggle loud, they leap and play,
Underneath the stars' ballet.

With each twist, they bump and fall,
Laughter echoes through the hall.
A rabbit snorts, a hedgehog sighs,
Oh, what fun beneath the skies!

As pomegranate juice drips near,
The bouncy shadows lend a cheer.
So join the dance, don't be shy,
Let's swirl like dreams before we fly.

Echoes of a Dusk-Embraced Dream

A furry fox with mischievous flair,
Painting clouds with a flick of hair.
His antics spark the twilight glow,
As whispers of adventure flow.

A chorus of crickets hums in tune,
While floating seeds drift like balloons.
Each shadow winks, a playful tease,
Dusk tickles night with gentle breeze.

The moon, a jester in the sky,
Winks at stars that giggle by.
With echoes of dreams upon the ground,
Laughter bounces, all around.

Through silken shadows, stories weave,
As playful spirits softly grieve.
Yet joy erupts, no need to pout,
Just let the dusk chase worries out.

Under the Gaze of Blushing Clouds

The clouds blush pink, a rosy hue,
As birds gossip about the dew.
They flip and flop, a funny show,
While wind tickles to and fro.

A lazy cat sprawls on the grass,
Chasing dreams as they softly pass.
Her whiskers twitch, she starts to pounce,
On fluffy clouds that seem to bounce.

A puppy hops, with socks mismatched,
Chasing shadows that have dispatched.
They tumble down, a burst of fun,
Underneath the blushing sun.

Giggles rise, a melody sweet,
As critters dance with wiggly feet.
Clouds blush bright, and so do we,
In this comedy of joy so free.

Tapestry of Evening's Hues

With threads of gold, the sun departs,
Spinning tales for silly hearts.
A patchwork dusk with colors bold,
As shadows dance, the night unfolds.

A dog in boots takes center stage,
Bounding 'round with joyful rage.
Each paw a splash of paint so fine,
On canvases of stars that shine.

A band of frogs croaks out a tune,
Singing praises to the moon.
With every ribbit, giggles flare,
As fireflies join in, unaware.

So let's paint the night with cheer,
And chase away the clouds of fear.
This tapestry, a playful sight,
Weaved from laughter, love, and light.

Golden Moments in the Orchard

In the orchard, apples roll,
Wobbling like a jolly troll.
Lemonade spills, oh what a sight,
As bees buzz by in pure delight.

A squirrel's dance upon a tree,
Lost its acorn, thinks it's free.
Peaches laugh, and cherries cheer,
While pumpkins plot their autumn beer.

Grapes hang tight in sunny beds,
Whispering secrets in their heads.
But watch your step, or you might fall,
Right into a peach brawl, after all!

Golden moments fill the air,
With giggles floating everywhere.
In this orchard, let's be wise:
Look out for fruit-shaped surprise pies!

A Tapestry of Twilight and Tropics

Evening creeps with a giggly grin,
As fireflies burst, then spin, and spin.
Lemons wear tiny hats so bright,
While coconuts dance left and right.

Mangoes burst into silly songs,
While parrots squawk, what's right, what's wrong.
On bananas, monkeys play,
Joking 'bout the end of the day.

Tropic winds with playful sways,
Breeze tickles plants, all in a craze.
Sunset's palette, a funny sight,
As pineapples chuckle, oh what a night!

Under stars, the laughter grows,
As silly jokes float like prose.
A tapestry woven of mirth,
Where humor finds its blessed worth.

Whispers of a Velvet Horizon

The horizon whispers silly tales,
Of quirky clouds and playful gales.
Watch the sun wearing shades so cool,
In this sky, we all feel like fools.

Stars peek out, twinkling with glee,
While the moon dances on a tree.
Crickets sing in rhyming spree,
As shadows play hide-and-seek with me.

A velvet quilt wraps the night tight,
While owls hoot jokes that take flight.
Laughter rides on the evening breeze,
With hints of mischief in the trees.

In this land of whimsical sight,
The whispers float, a sheer delight.
And when dawn breaks, we'll just sigh,
For the fun never says goodbye.

Secrets of a Sun-Kissed Twilight

Twilight spills secrets, full of cheer,
As shadows prance, not one, but sheer.
Marigolds gossip, sunflowers grin,
While crickets plot a ticklish win.

The breeze carries whispers of fun,
As children chase after the sun.
Fireflies flicker, a glitter parade,
While moonbeams shimmer, unafraid.

A bustling hedgehog writes a joke,
About a carrot, oh what a poke!
Candy-colored skies twist and turn,
As laughter ignites, a joyful burn.

Secrets softly eking their way,
Through the twilight at end of day.
With a wink and a nudge, we say,
Life's too short, let's laugh and play!

Tales from the Twilight Orchard

In the orchard where the gnomes dance,
The apples giggle, never miss a chance.
Worms wear hats and spin around,
While squirrels laugh, lost, but never found.

A pear once told a joke so sweet,
That the bees stopped buzzing to hear the beat.
Laughter erupted, trees shook with glee,
As fireflies blinked like stars on a spree.

A raccoon juggles cherries in the night,
While the moon snickers, hiding in sight.
Crickets chirp a tune quite bizarre,
Under the gaze of a winking star.

So if you wander near this place,
Bring a joke and a smile to embrace.
For in these twilight tales of mirth,
Laughter blossoms like the earth.

A Symphony of Starlit Fantasies

On a night where the giggles hum,
The stars sit back, tickled and numb.
A comet croaks a croaky song,
As cosmic clowns prance all night long.

Planets bounce like boisterous balls,
While Saturn trips and giggles, sprawls.
Jupiter holds a jump rope tight,
Counting moons as they soar in flight.

Nebulas twist in playful spins,
While black holes wink, betting on wins.
Galaxies bloom with chuckles and cheer,
As space dances, joking without fear.

So join the fun, don't be shy,
Under the wonders of the wide, wide sky.
For in this cosmic concert, so bright,
Every laugh shines like a starburst light.

Drifting in a Luminous Tide

In the ocean where the giggles flow,
Waves do the cha-cha, putting on a show.
Fish wear glasses, reading the deep,
While mermaids toss secrets they keep.

Seashells sing, their melodies wild,
Crabs wear shades, oh so styled.
Dolphins dance with a splash and a twirl,
As starfish giggle at the watery swirl.

The tide tickles toes on the shore,
Every wave whispers, 'Hey, want some more?'
Sandcastles bob, with smiles to share,
While every breeze carries laughter in air.

So let's ride the waves of this giddy tide,
With joy in our hearts and laughter as guide.
For in this sea of shimmering bright,
Every moment is dipped in light.

In the Embrace of Cosmic Whisper

In the hush where stardust plays,
Galactic giggles fill the maze.
Light years travel with a comical bounce,
While time itself does a goofy flounce.

Wormholes wink, making silly faces,
Moons throw pies in playful races.
Comets leave trails of sparkling tears,
As laughter echoes through cosmic spheres.

Black holes hide jokes, spinning so wide,
While constellations take a joy ride.
Twinkling stars join in the jest,
As the universe laughs, feeling so blessed.

So listen closely, let spirit rise,
In the quiet that shimmers, so wise.
For in this cosmic giggle and cheer,
Every whisper's a joke, loud and clear.

The Color of Dusk's Delight

As the sun starts to yawn, it turns quite peach,
Squirrels in bowties just out of reach.
Chasing shadows with wild glee,
While frogs compete in a sing-off spree.

Clouds mix colors like a child at play,
Dancing crumbs of light, a silly ballet.
An old owl snores, plus the goats just grin,
The whole forest giggles; it's where laughs begin.

The ants wear shades, strutting in line,
Planning a party for the nectar divine.
Grapes gossip softly, exchanging a glance,
While radishes rock out to a veggie dance!

Beetles tap-dance, oh what a sight,
As the evening blooms, warm and bright.
With each silly poke at the fading sun,
The breeze whispers secrets of joy and fun.

Petals and Pinks at Sundown

A pinky sky drapes over the hill,
While butterflies lounge, full and shrill.
Daisies crack jokes with their heads held high,
As mischievous ants make pies oh so spry.

The chubby bumblebees start to hum,
Bumping their bums as they go 'thrum-thrum.'
Time for the flowers to let out a toot,
While dandelions puff out their fuzzy suit!

A raccoon in sunglasses, oh what a sight,
Steals some ripe tomatoes, just for delight.
The fireflies giggle, winking on cue,
As we dance with the critters, so silly and true.

As petals turn dim under twilight's flirt,
Nectar spills laughter, sweet to the dirt.
The stars pop out to join in the play,
While evening chuckles, "What a fine day!"

Solstice Serenade Under Citrus Boughs

Lemons and limes gossip in the breeze,
While oranges tell tales, trying to tease.
The chickens are clucking with undeniable flair,
Cracking up jokes like they don't have a care.

As twilight approaches, the fruits get a glow,
A grapefruit winks, ready for the show.
A tiny mouse juggles seeds, oh what a view,
While owls sip jokes, brewing something new.

Squirrels burst forth in a playful race,
With a pinecone trophy, they claim their space.
While frogs serenade under branches so green,
A comedy club where no one's too keen!

The moon yells "Action!" oh what a cheer,
Citrus come alive, full of wonder and cheer.
The laughter echoes as night starts to play,
In this fruity circus, we dance the night away!

Lullabies from the Fruit-Laden Branches

Ripened fruits sway with a jolly hum,
Happily hanging, not feeling glum.
Each pear tells tales to the plump, sweet peach,
While cherries play poker, close enough to breach.

Kiwis strum softly, singing to the sky,
While apples join in, letting out a sigh.
The plums draw faces, making us roar,
As the laughter echoes through the orchard floor.

Frogs that ribbit in mismatched socks,
Hold a party where no one really talks.
The stars twinkle brightly, peeking to see,
What giggles and pokes are awaiting with glee.

As dusk wraps the trees in a cozy embrace,
Grasshoppers dance at their own silly pace.
Lullabies echo in this merry delight,
As we giggle with fruits till the fall of night.

Cradled by Lush Green Canopies

In a hammock strung between two trees,
I swayed with the breeze and giggled with ease.
A squirrel laughed loud, dropping acorns with glee,
While birds chattered secrets, just for me.

The leaves whispered tales of their wild little dance,
As I sipped my lemonade, lost in a trance.
A frog croaked a song, I swear it had flair,
And the shadows of insects seemed to float through the air.

Beneath the green laughter of branches so wide,
My worries crumbled like cookies beside.
I waved at a worm who wiggled in style,
He wiggled back, making my heart smile.

Swaying with nature, blissfully unaware,
Of squirrels that plotted to steal my cool chair.
But hey, who could fret when the world spins so bright?
In this verde parade, every moment feels right!

Flickering Fireflies in Evening's Embrace

Tiny lanterns flicker, dancing all about,
They twirl and they swirl, casting shadows, no doubt.
Chasing their glow, I stumbled and tripped,
A firefly winked, 'Don't you dare get whipped!'

In the twilight's giggle, I danced like a fool,
With the firefly brigade, I felt pretty cool.
Each flash a reminder to lighten my load,
While crickets provided the nighttime's sweet ode.

Caught up in the moment, with stars overhead,
I made silly wishes, like dancing to bread.
They twinkled and popped like popcorn in flight,
Sending giggles streaming into the night.

'Keep up!' called a firefly, as I paused just to stare,
Their laughter echoed, filling the air.
So I chased them with glee, through the meadow so wide,

Flickering wonders—my laughter-filled guide!

The Taste of Warm Breezes

Warm breezes tickle like a playful cat's paw,
In the garden of giggles, I'm filled with pure awe.
Each whisper of wind brings a fruity delight,
The nectar of sunshine makes everything bright.

I took a big breath, tasted highs and the lows,
Of sweetening petals and the dirt where it grows.
A honeybee buzzed like a joke that went loose,
He hummed 'Let's be friends, I'm just here for the juice!'

Lemonade sipped with a hint of the breeze,
I laughed with the daisies, swaying at ease.
The warmth wrapped around like a cozy old shawl,
Chasing butterflies, I felt ten feet tall.

The breeze told me jokes, and I giggled aloud,
While ants scurried past, feeling oh-so-proud.
With each gust I crowned, it was life's special prize,
As the sun dipped and danced in spectacular skies!

A Breath of Honeyed Air

With a rush of sweet air that tickled my nose,
I inhaled the giggles that flowered and rose.
The garden was bustling with nature's own cheer,
As I waded through laughter, oh so sincere.

The daisies were gossiping, spinning tall tales,
While bumblebees buzzed in their miniature gales.
They spoke of the weather and plans for a dance,
And I couldn't resist—I simply had to prance!

A soft warmth enveloped as I spun with delight,
Breezy jokes bounced through till the fall of the night.
The scents of the blossoms wrapped round like a hug,
As I twirled and I whirled, feeling bold as a bug.

So here's to the air, a breath sweet and light,
That fills me with giggles and dances at night.
In this garden of laughter where bees play their part,
Each sip of that sweetness fills joy in my heart!

A Garden of Ethereal Light

In the fields of cotton candy, all bright,
Squirrels wear tuxedos, oh what a sight!
Lemons laugh with limes, in a citrus ball,
While the clouds play hide and seek with us all.

Veggies dance jigs in this whimsical space,
Radishes twirl with a comical grace.
A parsnip with style, a carrot with flair,
Join the parade with no worry or care.

Under sprinkles of rainbows, we prance and slide,
Jellybeans giggle, with nowhere to hide.
With each silly breeze, laughter does soar,
In this garden of light, there's always more.

So come, take a trip, let your spirit run free,
Where the flowers are candy, as sweet as can be.
With gales full of chuckles, the air's full of cheer,
In this wondrous place, there's no room for fear.

Where Sweetness Meets the Sky

Cotton clouds pop, like gumdrops at play,
While raindrops tickle, and dance on the sway.
Chocolate rivers run sweet under sun,
In the land of giggles, we all have fun.

Caramel kites soar, across fruity hills,
A cream puff parade gives everyone thrills.
Lollipop trees sway, with laughter so bright,
As marshmallow critters join in for the night.

Sugary whispers float gently around,
As the moon, like a cookie, rolls off the ground.
Popcorn clouds burst, scattering joy in the air,
In this sweet, silly place, we dance without care.

So come grab a sprinkle, embrace the delight,
In our laughter-rimmed world, everything's right.
Join this scrumptious tale, let your worries fly,
For who can resist where sweetness meets sky?

Celestial Notes on a Raspberry Breeze

The stars all giggle in a raspberry wind,
Playing hula hoops with the planets, a trend.
Moonbeams strum melodies made out of light,
While comets wear hats, what a comical sight!

Galaxies twist in a jittery dance,
While stardust confetti falls, given a chance.
Each twirl and each spin has a giggle to share,
In the cosmos, you'll find a bright, playful flair.

Shooting stars whizz by, with witty remarks,
As nebulae swirl, making beautiful sparks.
A milky way fountain, frothy and bold,
Bubbles of laughter, stories untold.

So let the cosmos wrap you in glee,
With notes that echo, light as can be.
In this breezy realm, come join the fun,
For laughter is endless, all are welcome, everyone!

The Painted Veil of Afterglow

As sun dips low, colors dance in a whirl,
While the night shakes hands with a giggling pearl.
Pineapple fairies pirouette with delight,
Under this veil, stars twinkle goodnight.

With brushstrokes of laughter, the horizon glows,
As crickets compose tunes only the moon knows.
A caterpillar stands up to share jokes,
While owls swap puns with mischievous folks.

A carousel spins, lit by the soft gleam,
Of memories stitched in a whimsical dream.
Firefly lanterns blink, guiding the way,
Through giggles and whispers that dance and sway.

So embrace the oddity, let joy take its flight,
In this painted tale, everything's bright.
From dusk till dawn, let your spirit grow,
In the charm that's alive, of afterglow.

Whispers of the Painted Sky

Up above the clouds so shy,
A rabbit flips and waves goodbye.
He nibbles berries, oh so sweet,
While squirrels tap dance on their feet.

The sun drops low, a cheeky grin,
Chasing birds that fly to win.
Peaches spill from clouds of cream,
As laughter floats on whimsy's beam.

A painter's brush, with strokes so bold,
Sprinkles oranges and whispers gold.
While ants in hats parade around,
A jamboree of joy is found.

So come and laugh, join in the fun,
With giggles splashed beneath the sun.
In every hue, a joke will land,
A skyward circus, oh so grand.

Crescendo in the Twilight

The stars emerge, a twinkling show,
As fireflies flash, putting on a glow.
A raccoon plays a rusty drum,
While shadows dance, they wiggle, hum.

A cricket sings in lively tone,
Tickling the night, it's all his own.
Amidst the giggles, the owls do cheer,
For every note, a laugh draws near.

Each whispered breeze, a playful tease,
Tickles the leaves like a ticklish squeeze.
The moon winks down, a silver laugh,
In a twilight concert, a silly giraffe.

With jokes and jigs, the night does bloom,
As laughter fills the velvet room.
Join the night, let loose your sighs,
In mirthful echoes, the twilight flies.

Labyrinth of Blush and Gold

In tangled vines, where colors play,
The daisies laugh in bright dismay.
A chubby bumblebee rolls by,
With pollen pants, oh my, oh my!

The sunflowers giggle in a row,
As petals twirl in gleeful flow.
They ask the daisies, what's the plan?
For every flower dreams of a fan.

Through corridors of pink and zest,
The frogs engage in a jumpy fest.
Each leap a joke, each splash a cheer,
The laughter travels far and near.

In this maze of blush and gold,
Every secret flower has been told.
So take a stroll, let laughter lead,
In this silly garden, joy is freed.

The Cornucopia of Dusk's Palette

As dusk unfolds a fruit parade,
Bananas dance in a merry blade.
The grapes in capes roll down the hill,
While oranges play a zesty thrill.

A pineapple, with glasses slick,
Bounds around, a groovy trick.
As peaches blush in laughter sweet,
They cheer the rhythm of their beat.

The berries flaunt their juicy pride,
In swirling gowns they glide and slide.
With every twist, the colors scream,
In this cornucopia, we all dream.

So gather 'round as day takes flight,
In a riot of fruit, oh what a sight!
The laughter lingers in twilight's fall,
A whimsical feast for one and all.

The Poetry of Twilight's Embrace

As daylight dips, the shadows prance,
I met a frog who loves to dance.
He wore a hat, quite out of style,
And leaped with flair, oh what a smile!

The crickets chirp a silly tune,
While owls hold court with a silver spoon.
The stars poke fun, they twinkle bright,
As night unfolds, a giggling sight!

A rabbit juggles with carrots galore,
Claiming he's always wanted more.
With each toss, the veggies fly,
What a commotion under the sky!

And when the moon peeks with a grin,
I tip my hat and give a spin.
For in this time of evening play,
We celebrate the joy of our way!

Gilded Moments in a Sugarplum Sky

Clouds drape low, like fluffy cakes,
Where giggling fairies make some mistakes.
They fly too fast, bumping with glee,
Oh what a sight, that jolly spree!

A candy man walks with a lollipop hat,
Singing to folks, imagine that!
He spins his stick, a candy swirl,
Leaving the children in giggles and twirls.

The sun now dips, in raspberry hues,
While squirrels debate their favorite views.
They chatter and squeak, in quite the fuss,
Who saw the pie that was left on the bus?

When the stars burst forth like jellybeans,
The laughter echoes, the world convenes.
We dance till dawn, hearts all aglow,
In this sweet moment, together we grow!

Dappled Dreams under Candy-Coated Clouds

In a world where gumdrops fall,
Frolicking kittens heed the call.
They leap through puddles of purple rain,
Wearing tiny boots, oh what a gain!

A dragon flies with a candy cane,
Chasing his tail, quite a frame.
The sun chuckles, throwing golden beams,
As laughter ripples through our dreams.

The trees hum tunes with cookie bark,
While whispers flit from park to park.
Each bush sings soft with berries bright,
In this place where whimsy ignites.

As dusk descends, a party of stars,
We toast our cups filled with raspberry jars.
To moments sweet and laughter grand,
In this land where joy takes a stand!

Where Light Meets the Dreamer's Eye

In twilight's grip, the fireflies gleam,
With winks and blinks, they plot and scheme.
They twirl around in flickering flight,
Performing tricks that delight the night.

A jester's hat is perched on the moon,
While shadows dance to a merry tune.
The owls toast marshmallows, quite a fright,
Sharing giggles in the soft twilight.

Down by the brook, a beaver's tale,
Crafts a log boat fit to sail.
He tries to paddle with great charm,
But ends up in quite a splashy harm!

As laughter rings through every tree,
We celebrate, so wild and free.
This whimsical night, with laughter spun,
Where every gawk is a joke well done!

Rustling Leaves underneath a Shimmering Canopy

Leaves chatter gossip, oh so grand,
While squirrels plot their snack attack plan.
The sun peeks through, a golden tease,
As birds improvise a tune with ease.

A breeze tickles toes, laughter aloud,
While a lazy dog claims victory proud.
The branches sway with a playful dance,
As critters join in, taking a chance.

Caught in a game of tag with the sun,
Fluttering shadows, oh what fun!
With each rustling whisper, the trees conspire,
To keep the giggles from climbing higher.

Hints of mischief fly on a breeze,
Nature's comedy, a grand tease.
Under this cover, life's a delight,
Where grins and giggles take their flight.

Celestial Colors Over Ripened Fields

Fields adorned in patches of gold,
Where goofy scarecrows strike a pose bold.
Bumblebees bust a move, oh so sweet,
While clouds gather, planning a soup to eat.

The horizon winks in a riot of hues,
As mischievous winds play dress-up with shoes.
Each ear of corn whispers a secret dream,
While rabbits plot a grasshopper theme.

Sunflowers giggle in the amber glow,
Under a party sky, they steal the show.
A comet zips by, sporting a grin,
Sending twinkling wishes, let the fun begin!

With a chortle of thunder, jokes take flight,
As stars join in the late-night light.
Fields of laughter, all creatures unite,
Painting the world in sheer delight.

The Sweetness of Dusk's Palette

As day bids adieu with a wink and a smile,
Fireflies practice their dance all the while.
A breeze hums softly, a lullaby tune,
While the moon polishes silver to swoon.

Pink cotton candy dreams fill the air,
While crickets engage in a humorous flare.
Courageous frogs leap, sharing their tales,
While twilight whispers, "Let's ride the gales!"

Stars are forming a line for a show,
Each one with stories they're eager to blow.
A painted sky with a ticklish hue,
Where dusk unveils laughter, and giggles renew.

In the sweetness of dusk, we gather and play,
With chuckles and warmth, we chase fears away.
Nature's canvas spills joy, wild and free,
A spectacle painted for you and for me.

Chasing Shadows through Sun-Drenched Dreams

In sunny patches, shadows jump high,
While giggling children let their dreams fly.
With goofy hats made from the grass,
Running in circles like a spun sugar mass.

Each tiny footstep leaves bursts of mirth,
On this playground of magic, we find our worth.
The sun winks down, playing hide and seek,
With shadows dancing, cheeky and sleek.

Pigs twirl in mud, looking for fame,
While frogs croak along—they're all in the game.
A slicing breeze brings a soft little tease,
As laughter erupts, dancing through trees.

With dreams wrapped in sunlight, we chase and we run,
Through the fields where mischief is never outdone.
Shadows of joy, racing to tomorrow,
In this realm of laughter, we banish sorrow.

Secrets of the Sun-Kissed Canopy

In the treetops, squirrels prance,
Chasing shadows, lost in dance.
Lemons giggle, oranges sigh,
While bananas wave us goodbye.

Under beams of golden light,
Laughter echoes, pure delight.
Pick a pear, try to make it sing,
A fruity choir, let joy take wing.

Jellybeans grow on vines so high,
Polar bears just help them fly.
A watermelon drips with cheer,
Telling jokes no one can hear.

Here in this lush, silly place,
Fruit and fun embrace with grace.
Nutty antics all around,
In this grove, joy knows no bound.

Dreams in a Fruitful Grove

Once I dreamed of a peach parade,
With dancing apples, unafraid.
Pineapples twirled, so spry and bright,
While grapes in hats laughed in delight.

The cherry trees wore lilac socks,
Popping jokes like playful clocks.
Mangoes juggled, making a scene,
Avocados rolled with glee unseen.

In this grove where giggles bloom,
Fruits all spill from nature's womb.
Lay back, watch a kiwi fly,
No need for rules when fruits can try.

The sun set low, a silly show,
Fruits take bows, pausing just so.
In dreams, we dance, we laugh, we sing,
In this world, all good fruits swing.

Reflections of a Starlit Garden

Beneath the moon, flowers chatter,
Sweet peas gossip, oh, what a matter!
Lettuce laughs at the night so bright,
While daisies flirt with the starry light.

A pond of jelly wobbles and sways,
While radishes offer comedic ways.
Cabbages whisper, secrets in tune,
Under a chuckling, glowing moon.

Twilight teases, painting the scene,
With vine-swinging veggies, oh so green.
Carrots tell tales of the sun and rain,
In this garden, fun reigns again.

Bumblebees swirl like fluffy balloons,
Tickling the cosmos with little tunes.
In this starlit realm, all worries cease,
Nature giggles, inviting peace.

The Blooming Mirage

In a meadow of laughter, flowers play,
Bouncing petals, a whimsical ballet.
Tulips wiggle, and daisies spin,
Silly butterflies begin to grin.

Cacti boast of their prickly charm,
While laughing oaks raise their arm.
Bees sport hats, so fashionably bright,
Pollinating puns in the gold-filled light.

A mirage blooms with candy canes,
Bubbly saplings break all chains.
Fields of laughter serve sweet delight,
As earth joins in on the playful night.

In a world where giggles grow,
Every joke is a fruit to sow.
As stars wink down, all troubles fade,
In this blooming mirage, we've got it made.

Radiant Threads on a Canvas of Dreams

In a world where clouds wear hats,
Laughter spills from lazy cats.
Colors dance on threads so bright,
Chasing the giggles into the night.

A canvas swirls with bubblegum,
Where rainbows hum and cupcakes drum.
Silly shadows jump and play,
Painting joy in a wacky way.

The sun wears shades, a cheeky grin,
As banana boats sail with a spin.
Buttons bounce and spoons do whirl,
In this vibrant, fun-filled world.

With each stroke, the canvas gleams,
A playful place, a land of dreams.
Silly stories yet untold,
In laughter's arms, we find our gold.

When the Evening Blooms

As twilight giggles, stars peek out,
Fireflies waltz, without a doubt.
The moon, a pie, so round and keen,
Whispers secrets, a silvery scene.

Crickets chirp their tune so sweet,
While sneaky breezes wiggle at our feet.
Night unfolds in a twinkling show,
Twirling colors, oh, how they glow!

Jelly beans drop from the sky,
And donuts roll as if to fly.
Under laughter, the evening blooms,
Painting joy with candy fumes.

Each moment sparkles, no room for gloom,
As silliness fills the vibrant room.
In dreams, we bounce, we float, we sway,
In the evening's fun, we want to stay.

The Dance of Sunset Swirls

Where the sun spins in a purple tux,
And the clouds giggle with silly plucks.
Cotton candy floats on breezy waves,
As shadows sway in their crispy grades.

The horizon tickles with playful hues,
While laughter echoes in crazy snooze.
Dancing daisies wiggle and twine,
In a ballet, they twist and shine.

As the day yawns and the stars align,
We join the dance, a goofy line.
With every twirl, a chuckle blooms,
Creating joy in colorful rooms.

So come along, let's laugh and sway,
In the sunset's giggle, we want to play.
With swirling colors, our spirits soar,
In this funny dance, forever more!

Between the Hues of Strawberry and Peach

In a garden where laughter grows wild,
Strawberries giggle, sweet like a child.
Peaches blush with ticklish delight,
As they sway in the warm sunlight.

Bubblegum breezes lift us high,
While we play hide and seek with the sky.
Frolicking frogs wear tiny crowns,
Jumping around in magical towns.

Fruits play tag in a juicy race,
With every tickle, they switch their place.
Colors collide in a fruity hush,
Crafting a world that makes us blush.

So let's dance where the flavors meet,
In a silly game, oh what a treat!
Between the hues, we skip and sway,
In laughter's garden, we'll forever play.

A Canvas of Soft Hues

In the morning, colors dance,
Giggling clouds in a sky's prance.
Lemons roll and oranges skip,
A fruity laugh, a playful trip.

Mangoes toss in a breeze's play,
Cheeky whispers on sunny display.
Watermelons giggle as they roll,
Each slice a joke, a juicy stroll.

Peaches shimmy in the bright light,
Bouncing around, oh what a sight!
Grapes tickle with their tiny glee,
In this world, fruit is wild and free.

Underneath those playful beams,
Nature swirls with whimsical dreams.
A canvas bright with laughter bloomed,
Where grinning fruits are joyfully zoomed.

The Serenity of Sweet Fruits and Skies

On a hill, the berries flirt,
With a soft breeze in their shirt.
Kiwi sings as it plucks a string,
Raspberries dance, oh what a fling!

Pineapple hats wave in the air,
As oranges play without a care.
Bananas slip on a sunlit stage,
Creating giggles at every age.

A cherry wink, a peachy grin,
Nature's comedy, where to begin?
Juicy laughter fills the air,
Beneath the tableau, troubles wear.

In this orchard of funny cheer,
Everyone gathers, far and near.
A giggling feast, oh can't resist,
Sweet fruits and skies, you get the gist!

Where the Sun Meets the Fertile Earth

In fields of smiles, the melons play,
Sunbeams tickling them all the way.
Tomatoes chuckle in rows so neat,
While peas do silly dances on their feet.

Cucumbers stretch in the warm delight,
As radishes hide, just out of sight.
A garden of fun with a fruity jest,
Laughter grows, a happy quest.

Carrots peek from their beds so snug,
With mischievous eyes, they give a tug.
Eggplants grin, their purple hue,
In this patch, hilarity brews.

The sun dips low with a playful wink,
Beneath its glow, the veggies think.
A harvest of laughter, joy, and mirth,
Where giggles sprout from the fertile earth.

Twilight Hues in Nature's Gallery

Twilight comes, the sky's in a spin,
As the fruits giggle, beguiled by the din.
Apples snicker as stars appear,
In twilight's hue, they dance with cheer.

Plums in jackets so purple and bright,
Swing to the rhythm of the night.
Cherries blush in the soft twilight,
Under the blanket of the sky's light.

A laugh from a pumpkin, quite the sight,
While zucchinis plan their next flight.
In this gallery of vibrant views,
Nature's laughter paints twilight hues.

In the quiet, the jokes intertwine,
As laughter ripples through vines so fine.
Twilight grows, and aromas swirl,
In a fruity comedy, they laugh and twirl.

Stars Tangle in Melodic Whispers

Twinkling lights in a dance so bright,
Cats plotting mischief, what a sight.
The moon keeps giggling, strumming a tune,
While fireflies join in, wearing hats from June.

Bouncing through shadows, laughter abounds,
Tacos in hand, we twirl round and round.
The constellations wink, sharing a joke,
As a cow jumps over, and then it just chokes.

Jellybeans scatter on the cool grass,
While frogs serenade, with elegance, sass.
Each crickets' chirp is a ticklish thrill,
As we share silly secrets, heartbeats to still.

In the kaleidoscope night, we smile and cheer,
Chasing the stars, without a single fear.
Who knew the cosmos could burst out in song,
Under the blanket where giggles belong.

Cradled in the Arms of Dusk

As daylight dips into a comical haze,
Squirrels swap stories of nutty escapades.
With a wink from the sun, the day takes a bow,
Even the shadows seem to giggle somehow.

Lollipops hanging from branches so low,
Bringing sweet laughter as breezes blow.
In families of owls, wisdom takes flight,
But mostly they nap through the magical night.

Dusk wraps us snug, like a big fluffy hug,
While fireflies hiccup and give us a shrug.
Stars tumble out, like kids in a race,
No space left empty in this whimsical space.

As darkness settles, we munch on delight,
Beneath fluttering whispers, we dance till it's light.
With cheeks full of giggles, our spirits ignite,
In this cheeky embrace, everything feels right.

Kaleidoscope Dreams of the Night

Colors collide in the twilight's embrace,
A rainbow of laughter on every face.
Fireflies paint pictures across the night sky,
While a sleepy dog dreams of chasing a pie.

Confetti of stars, a mischievous tease,
Whispering chuckles in the cool evening breeze.
As we twirl and spin, we swirl into schemes,
Dreaming of cake and a world made of dreams.

In pajamas adorned with bright dancing snacks,
The night wears a grin as we plan our attacks.
Crickets in chorus, a raucous delight,
While shadows pirouette, embracing the night.

With giggles and mischief, we dive and we sway,
In a kaleidoscope swirl, we're light on our way.
Each moment a burst of absurdity's cheer,
As we tumble through dreams that feel almost near.

The Twilight's Sweet Serenade

Notes from the twilight drift soft on the air,
As giggles explode without a moment's care.
Chasing the shadows, we wink at the trees,
While night's playful whisper carries our pleas.

The laughter of crickets fills up the night sky,
A symphony brewed on a raspberry pie.
In a world where pranks dance on the moonlit floor,
We jest and we jive, and we always want more.

Each star tells a mystery wrapped up in bright fun,
As a squirrel tries cartwheels, competing with the sun.
Fireflies flash like confetti in flight,
While we giggle between bites of chocolate delight.

With the backdrop of dusk painting everything right,
We waltz through our dreams, keeping worries in fright.
In this serenade, where hearts sing and play,
We savor each moment, as twilight gives way.

Harmonics of the Twilight Spectrum

In a jumbled jive, the stars go bop,
The moon sticks out a leg and does a hop.
Crickets chirp in a tune so sweet,
While fireflies dance on tiny feet.

The clouds wear hats, a silly sight,
As night unfolds in pure delight.
With a wink, the night sings a tune,
"Come join us for a waltz, you loon!"

Planets giggle, oh what a sound,
As stardust flutters all around.
Galaxies spin in a playful game,
Even the dark gets caught in fame.

So grab your socks, let's join the dance,
A nocturnal bash, what a chance!
Laugh with the night, be merry and bright,
For fun awaits in this starry night.

An Ode to the Wandering Stars

Oh wandering lights, you cosmic clowns,
Roaming the sky in fluffy gowns.
Twinkle, twirl, what a sight to see,
As you giggle down at you and me.

With silly grins and halos too,
You pop out jokes like morning dew.
Each sparkle is a chuckle, a tease,
Making wishes float on the breeze.

Constellations bicker, a playful fight,
As orbs of chaos make things right.
While comets swoop in to steal the show,
Leaving trails of laughter where'er they go.

So raise a glass to the roaming crew,
For silliness beams in every hue.
With starlit puns lighting the way,
You turn the night into pure play.

Chasing Dreams through Starry Foliage

In a forest of wishes, we chase and scoot,
Dodging tricky shadows where giggles hoot.
Branches sway low, just to tease,
Whispering secrets carried by the breeze.

Shooting stars hide behind leaves,
Sharing jokes only the night believes.
With every rustle, a chuckle springs,
As owls collect the tales that night brings.

Bouncing off logs and stumps like springs,
We dance with the night, oh the joy it brings!
Each step a twirl, each laugh a cheer,
In this realm of dreams, we've nothing to fear.

So let's twirl through the cool, green maze,
Laugh 'till dawn in this playful haze.
For under the stars, we're free to roam,
In the woods of wonder, we find our home.

Colors of the Evening Blossom

Hues of purple and pink, what a show,
The sky blooms brightly, as if in a throw.
With laughter swirling in every shade,
Night's canvas dances, unafraid.

Tickled by twilight's brush, we sway,
Colors giggle in a vibrant array.
The horizon tips its hat with cheer,
Saying, "Join the fun, the night is near!"

Pinks and blues, they bump and blend,
Playful shades on which we depend.
As laughter rises from every crevice,
The calm of night, a silly promise.

So tiptoe through this painted dream,
Where colors laugh and giggles beam.
For the evening blossom, wild and free,
Is a party for you, and also for me.

When the Heavens Turn Silken

In the garden where thoughts collide,
A cat wears shades as a sun's guide.
Lemons giggle in the afternoon glow,
While dancing shoes twirl to and fro.

The raspberries plan a parade of fluff,
They're all dressed up; oh, isn't that tough?
Clouds throw confetti, the sky starts to wink,
As squirrels toss acorns, not missing a beat.

With rabbits in top hats, all quite absurd,
They juggle their dreams, their tails in a whirl.
Sunsets laugh softly, painting the scene,
A chorus of crickets in evening's routine.

As stars become hiccups, all sparkle and shine,
The moon, like a dancer, begins to recline.
In the silken glow, laughter takes flight,
In the evening's embrace, everything's right.

Reflections of a Charmed Abyss

Mirrors of whimsy, a pool by the gate,
Frogs wear tuxedos, yet seem quite late.
Fish in bow ties swim by so fast,
Chasing their tails, it's a comical blast.

The old willow tree leans with a grin,
Whispering secrets, as shadows spin.
A raccoon in glasses reads tales of bliss,
While fireflies giggle at a sly little kiss.

Under the moon, the owls have a feast,
While foxes play chess, it's fun, at least!
The night sky chuckles, a riddle divine,
As starlight spills over, in whimsical line.

Songs of whimsy echo and dance,
Life's a funny dream, a pure happenstance.
So join in the laughter, take a quick pass,
In reflections of joy, we all raise a glass!

Beneath the Citrus Veil

In a grove where laughter ripens and sways,
Lemons and limes have fun-filled days.
Oranges giggle, they roll down the hill,
While a grapefruit jokes, 'I'm such a thrill!'

The bees play the banjo, a sweet little tune,
As birds wear hats, strut under the moon.
Mangoes tease grapes, 'We're juicier, friend!'
While cherries blush red, and their laughs never end.

A picnic unfolds on a plaid blanket spread,
With sandwiches doing the cha-cha instead.
Peaches sip soda, y'all better believe,
In this zestful world, it's hard not to grieve.

As twilight begins, with a sprinkle of cheer,
The fruits share their tales; everyone's near.
This citrusy jubilee won't fade away,
In the laughter of orchards, we twirl and sway.

The Last Embrace of Daylight

When the sun takes a bow, all tired and done,
Crickets whisper secrets, day's been such fun.
The clouds wear pajamas; they snuggle so tight,
While stars play tag in the velvet of night.

A dog on a swing sings to a passing kite,
As ants throw a party under the moonlight.
The breeze tells a joke to the kite in the sky,
And the trees hold their breath, letting laughter fly.

In the bathtub of dusk, the frogs start to croak,
While shadows escape with a delicate poke.
Fireflies sketch doodles, tails add a dash,
As raccoons recite lines, a wild, charming clash.

In the warm glow of evening, a symphony plays,
With giggles and whispers, a wondrous ballet.
As the last hue of daylight bids all goodnight,
Laughter will linger, till the dawn brings the light.

www.ingramcontent.com/pod-product-compliance
Lightning Source LLC
Chambersburg PA
CBHW051735290426
43661CB00123B/438